Material Matters

Mixtures, Compounds & Solutions

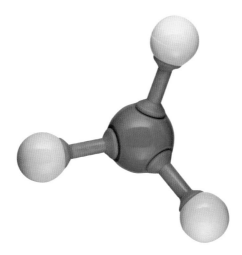

Carol Baldwin

www.raintreepublishers.co.uk
Visit our website to find out more information about **Raintree** books.

To order:
☎ Phone 44 (0) 1865 888113
▤ Send a fax to 44 (0) 1865 314091
▢ Visit the Raintree Bookshop at **www.raintreepublishers.co.uk** to browse our catalogue and order online.

First published in Great Britain by Raintree Publishers, Halley Court, Jordan Hill, Oxford, OX2 8EJ, part of Harcourt Education Ltd.
Raintree is a registered trademark of Harcourt Education Ltd.

Produced for Raintree Publishers by Discovery Books Ltd.
Editorial: Louise Galpine, Carol Usher, Charlotte Guillain, and Isabel Thomas
Design: Victoria Bevan, Keith Williams (sprout.uk.com Limited), and Michelle Lisseter
Picture Research: Maria Joannou and Alison Prior
Production: Duncan Gilbert and Jonathan Smith
Index: Indexing Specialists (UK) Ltd
Printed and bound in China by South China Printing Company
Originated by Dot Gradations Ltd

ISBN 1 844 43601 2 (hardback)
09 08 07 06 05
10 9 8 7 6 5 4 3 2 1

ISBN 1 844 43686 1 (paperback)
09 08 07 06 05
10 9 8 7 6 5 4 3 2 1

British Library Cataloguing in Publication Data
Baldwin, Carol, 1943-
Mixtures, compounds and solutions. – (Freestyle express. Material matters)
1. Chemistry – Juvenile literature 2. Mixtures – Juvenile literature
546

A full catalogue record for this book is available from the British Library.

This levelled text is a version of Freestyle: Material Matters: Mixtures, Compounds & Solutions.

Photo acknowledgements
Page 7, 20, 31, 41 Tudor Photography; 21, Art Directors & Trip; 42–43, Art Directors & Trip/ H Rogers; 30, Art Directors & Trip/M Walker; 6–7,8–9, 10, 11, 12, 14, 22–23, 24, 34, 36–37, 38–39, Corbis; 24–25, Corbis/Bettmann; 34–35, Corbis/C Cohen; 20–21, Corbis/D Pebbles; 29, Corbis/G Lepp; 44, Corbis/G Lepp; 18, Corbis/J L Pelaez; 28–29, Corbis/ K Fleming; 43, Corbis/L Bergman; 30–31, Corbis/L Lefkowitz; 19, Corbis/M Gerber; 33, Corbis/O Franken; 25, Corbis/P Souders; 40–41, Corbis/S Agliolo; 15, Corbis/Vanni Archive; 9, Corbis/W White; 10–11, Empics; 6, FLPA; 5 bottom, FLPA/Foto Natura Catalogue; 35, FLPA/Foto Natura Catalogue; 4, FLPA/Maurice Nimmo; 32–33, FLPA/Minden Pictures; 17, FLPA/R Brooks; 22, FLPA/Robin Chittenden; 19, FLPA/W Meinderts; 27, FLPA/W Wisniewski; 4–5,8, 14–15, 23 Geophotos/ T Waltham; 5 top,16–17, 36,40,45, Photodisc; 37, Science Photo Library; 38, Science Photo Library; 16, Science Photo Library/ Adam Hart Davis; 12–13, Science Photo Library/CNRI; 39, Science Photo Library/Earth Satellite Corporation; 42, Science Photo Library/Mark Thomas; 5 middle, 26–27, Science Photo Library/ Prof S Cinti/CNRI; 28, Trevor Clifford

Cover photograph reproduced with permission of Topham Picturepoint.

Contents

Any words appearing in the text in bold, **like this**, are explained in the Glossary. You can also look out for some of them in the Word bank at the bottom of each page.

Climbing high

Granite
This is a piece of red granite. You can see the tiny bits or **particles** that make up the rock. Dark bits are mixed together with light bits.

Half Dome is a huge dome of granite rock. It is in the Yosemite National Park, California, USA. Half Dome is 1462 metres (4752 feet) high. Many people visit the Yosemite Valley each year and see the rock. But how many people think about what the rock is made of?

All rocks are **mixtures** of **minerals**. Most granite is made up of tiny bits of the minerals quartz, mica, and feldspar.

Granite from Half Dome is different to granite from other places. This is because granite is a mixture.

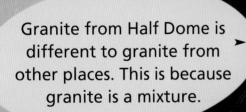

Word bank   mineral non-living solid material

Compounds and mixtures

The minerals in rocks are chemical **compounds**. This means they are made from different types of **atoms** or tiny particles joined together. The atoms in mixtures come together too, but they do not join up. Most rocks are mixtures of compounds.

Solutions

Pure water is a compound. But most water has other materials mixed with it. Then water is a special type of mixture. It is a **solution**.

Find out later ...

... what is made when the Space Shuttle lifts off.

... what compound is found in your stomach.

... how can fish suffocate in water.

Describing matter

Five kinds of matter
The ancient Chinese thought that there were five kinds of matter. These were fire, wood, metal, earth, and water.

Matter is everywhere. Anything that takes up space and has **mass** is matter. The more mass something has, the heavier it is. Matter can either be a **pure substance** or a **mixture**.

A pure substance is the same throughout. Water and other **compounds** are pure substances. Mixtures do not have the same features throughout. Granite is a mixture. Some parts of granite have more dark **particles** than other parts.

Word bank   mass amount of matter in an object

Elements

Compounds and mixtures are made up of **elements**. Elements are made of only one type of **atom**. They are the purest type of matter. Carbon is an element.

States of matter

Matter can take different forms. Most matter can be solid, liquid, or gas. These forms are called the **states of matter**.

Is this glass only two-thirds full?
No! This glass is full. Part of the glass that does not contain orange juice contains air. Air is a mixture of invisible gases.

An iceberg is water in its solid state. Solids keep the same shape.

Orange juice is a liquid. It takes the shape of the glass.

Physical properties

Everything around us has features that help us to see what it is. Copper is an **element**. A piece of copper wire is shiny-orange, and will bend. Chalk is a **compound**. A piece of chalk will break easily because it is **brittle**. It is white and dull. Parts of a **mixture**, such as sand and pebbles, have different colours, shapes, and sizes. So you can easily tell them apart.

Colour, brittleness, and smoothness are some **physical properties**. You can usually tell these by looking or measuring.

Glowing rocks
Some minerals glow when **ultraviolet (UV) light** shines on them. This is a physical property.

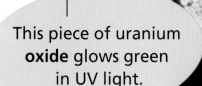

This piece of uranium **oxide** glows green in UV light.

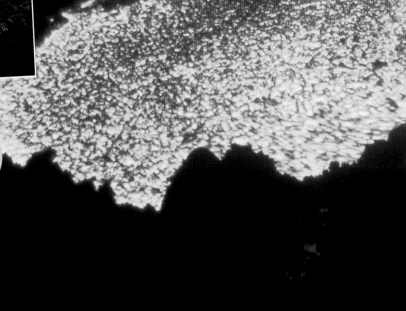

brittle firm to touch but easy to break

Physical changes

If you break a piece of chalk, its size and shape changes. Some of its physical properties have changed. But it is still chalk. A change in size or shape is a **physical change**.

A change in **state of matter** is also a physical change. When water **boils** or **freezes**, it is still water. When ice **melts** and changes from a solid to a liquid, it is still water. These physical changes do not change what makes up water.

Very very hot!
Diamonds have a very high **melting point**. The temperature must reach 3550 °C (6440 °F). Then a diamond will melt. This is two-thirds as hot as the surface of the Sun!

When a volcano **erupts**, hot, liquid rock pours out. This is called lava. When lava cools, it changes back to solid rock. This change of state is a physical change.

physical property feature that can be seen or measured without changing what a substance is made of

Chemical properties

When a substance is with another substance it may **react**. A **chemical property** tells us what will happen. Iron reacts with oxygen in damp air to form **rust**. This is a chemical property of iron.

A chemical property of fuels, such as petrol and coal, is that they burn easily. Some **metals**, like calcium and zinc, react with **acids**. This is a chemical property of calcium and zinc.

Autumn colours

In autumn the leaves on some trees change colour. This is because the chemical that makes them green changes. A colour change is one sign of a chemical change.

chemical property feature of something that tells us how it will react

Chemical changes

A chemical change takes place when iron reacts with oxygen. A new substance is formed. This is called iron **oxide** or rust. This change is called a **chemical reaction**. The rust is a new substance with new **properties**.

Elements, **compounds**, and **mixtures** all take part in chemical reactions.

Petrol burns in a racing car engine. This is a chemical property of petrol. It gives off **energy** to make the engine run.

Crazy colours

To get colour changes like this you have to use hair colouring kits. These kits contain three special chemicals. These chemicals react with the hair and change the hair's natural colour.

---

chemical reaction change that produces one or more new substances

Building blocks of matter

The Ancient Greeks decided that you could not keep on dividing **matter** forever. At some point you would reach the smallest piece. They named this smallest piece an **atom**. It means "cannot be divided".

In the early 1800s, John Dalton came up with some ideas about matter:

- all **elements** are made from atoms
- atoms cannot be divided or destroyed
- atoms of the same element are all the same
- atoms of different elements are different
- atoms of two or more elements can join to form **compounds**.

Atomic power

Today we can split the atom into even smaller particles. This releases huge amounts of **energy**. It is called nuclear energy. We can see this when an atom bomb explodes.

Word bank   nucleus centre of an atom, made of protons and neutrons

Smaller particles in an atom

All matter is made of atoms. An atom has a centre part. This is called a **nucleus**. The nucleus is made of two kinds of **particle**. **Protons** are particles with a positive **charge**. **Neutrons** are particles that have no charge.

Electrons are a third kind of particle in an atom. They have a negative charge. In an atom the number of electrons is the same as the number of protons. The charges balance. So overall the atom has no charge.

Where are the electrons?

Electrons are arranged around the nucleus. They are in different energy levels or shells. Each energy level can only hold a certain number of electrons before it becomes full.

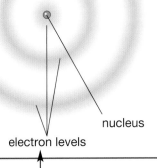

nucleus

electron levels

It would take a million atoms lined up in a row to be the same thickness as a human hair.

This diagram shows where scientists think electrons are in an atom.

electron tiny, negatively charged particle outside the nucleus of an atom

Identifying elements

An **element** is made from only one type of **atom**. There are three main groups of elements.

Metals

Most elements, such as iron, are **metals**. Nearly all metals are solids. Only mercury is a liquid at **room temperature**.

All metals can look shiny. Heat and electricity move well through metals. Many metals can be stretched into wires. They can be hammered or shaped without breaking.

Metal ores

Metals are often found in rocks, called **ores**. Haematite is an ore. It is a compound of iron and oxygen. We mine haematite to get iron.

This **geyser** is in Yellowstone National Park, USA. It has sulphur around its edge. Sulphur is a yellow non-metal element.

non-metal element without the properties of metals

Non-metals

Most **non-metals** are gases, such as nitrogen. Some are solids, such as carbon. Diamonds are a form of carbon. Bromine is the only non-metal that is liquid at room temperature. Non-metals are not shiny. Heat and electricity do not pass through them easily. Solid non-metals usually break if they are hammered. They are **brittle**.

Metalloids

A few elements have **properties** of both metals and non-metals. They are called **metalloids**.

Symbols of elements
Chemical symbols are a short way of writing the names of elements. Symbols have one or two letters. The first is always a capital letter.

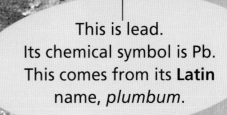

This is lead. Its chemical symbol is Pb. This comes from its **Latin** name, *plumbum*.

metalloid element with some properties of both metals and non-metals

Compounds

Compounds are made of **atoms** of more than one **element**. Water is a compound. It is made of hydrogen and oxygen atoms. The atoms in a compound are joined tightly together.

Combining elements

Elements only join together to make compounds if there is a **chemical reaction**. When small pieces of iron are mixed with sulphur powder you get a **mixture**. A chemical change only happens if the mixture is heated. Then a compound called iron **sulphide** forms.

This is a model of the compound ammonia. The white balls are hydrogen atoms and the blue ball is a nitrogen atom.

compound substance made of two or more different types of atom joined together

Properties of compounds

Compounds do not have the **properties** of the elements they contain.

Sugar is a white solid with a sweet taste. Sugar is a compound of hydrogen, oxygen, and carbon. Carbon is a black solid. Hydrogen and oxygen are both gases with no colour. Hydrogen, oxygen, and carbon are very different to sugar.

The Space Shuttle used aluminium powder as a fuel. Aluminium joins up with oxygen. The compound aluminium oxide is formed.

Please pass the salt
Sodium is a bright, silvery **metal**. It explodes when it **reacts** with water. Chlorine is a **poisonous** gas. But they react together to form white **crystals** of sodium chloride, or salt.

Carbon and oxygen

Carbon usually burns in air and when there is plenty of oxygen. Then carbon dioxide, CO_2, is formed. Carbon also burns when there is not enough oxygen. Then carbon monoxide, CO, is made.

A **compound** is always made up of the same **elements**. Also the **atoms** always join up in the same way. If they join in a different way, a different compound forms.

Water has two hydrogen atoms to every oxygen atom. But hydrogen and oxygen can join in a different way to this. Two atoms of hydrogen can join with two atoms of oxygen. This forms a compound called hydrogen peroxide. Water and hydrogen peroxide are very different. Hydrogen peroxide is used to kill **bacteria** on cuts and to **bleach** hair.

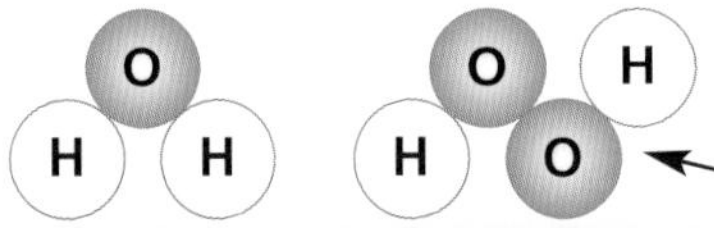

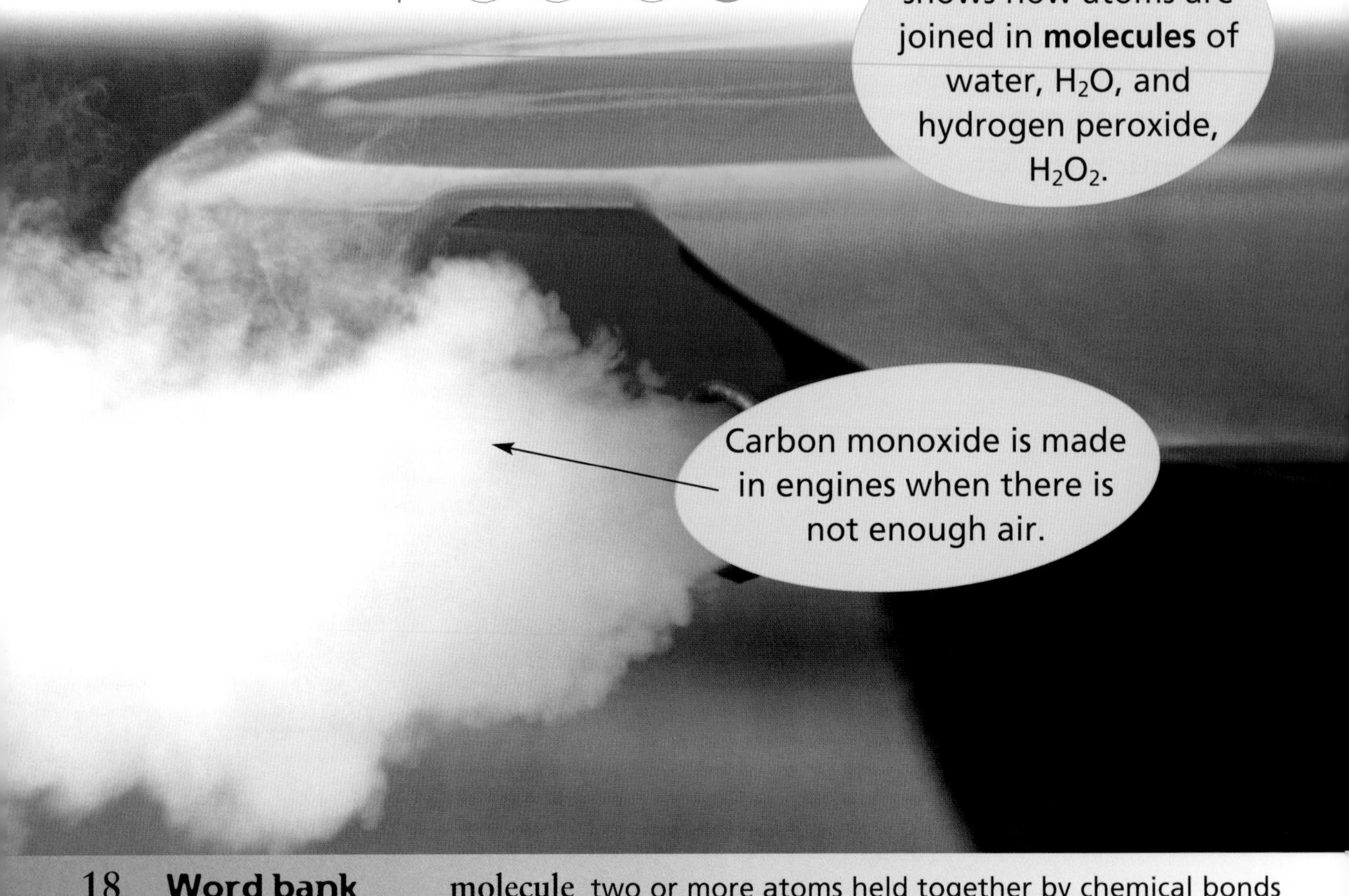

This diagram shows how atoms are joined in **molecules** of water, H_2O, and hydrogen peroxide, H_2O_2.

Carbon monoxide is made in engines when there is not enough air.

molecule two or more atoms held together by chemical bonds

Breaking elements apart

You can break compounds apart. But you need a **chemical reaction** to do this. **Energy** is often needed to make a reaction happen. This could be heat, light, or electricity. If you heat sugar strongly, it causes a chemical change. It breaks the sugar apart. If you heat sugar for long enough, only black carbon will be left. The hydrogen and oxygen join to form **water vapour**. This goes off into the air.

Living things, like mushrooms and moulds, are decomposers.

Decomposers

There are lots of compounds in dead plants and animals. These will break down into elements and simpler compounds. Living things called decomposers are able to help do this.

Hydrogen peroxide can make brown hair blonde.

Chemical bonds

Atoms are tightly joined together when they make a **compound**. **Chemical bonds** form between them. But not all chemical bonds are the same. Compounds belong to two different groups. These are based on their chemical bonds.

Covalent bonds

In some compounds the atoms share **electrons** in a bond. These are called **covalent compounds**. Water is a covalent compound.

Harmful chemicals

Covalent compounds can be harmful. They turn into a gas readily. Many also burn easily. Covalent compounds are often used in nail polish remover.

Uses: As a fuel for burners and as a household solvent. Harmful by inhalation, in contact with skin and if swallowed. Harmful: possible risk of irreversible effects through inhalation, in contact with skin and if swallowed. Keep locked up and out of the reach of children. Keep container tightly closed. Keep away from sources of ignition – No smoking. Wear suitable protective clothing and gloves. In case of accident or if you feel unwell seek medical advice immediately (show the label where possible). Contains Methanol.

HARMFUL

HIGHLY FLAMMABLE

Products that are dangerous have warnings on their labels.

chemical bond strong attraction between two atoms

Ions and ionic bonds

Metals join with **non-metals**. The metal gives one or more electrons to the non-metal. Sodium is a metal. Chlorine is a non-metal. When they join, sodium chloride, or salt is formed. Each sodium atom gives an electron to a chlorine atom.

When sodium chloride forms, the sodium atom loses an electron. It has a positive charge. It is called a sodium **ion**. The chlorine atom takes an electron. It has a negative charge and is called a chloride ion.

Crystals

These are **crystals** of salt, or sodium chloride. Each crystal contains sodium and chloride ions.

Both the water and sand in this picture are covalent compounds.

ion atom or group of atoms with an electric charge

Nitrogen oxides

There are a few different nitrogen **oxides**. They are all gases. Nitrogen oxide, NO, comes from car exhausts. Dentists use dinitrogen oxide, N_2O, to relax patients. It is also called "laughing gas".

Chemical formula

All **elements** have a **chemical symbol**. These symbols are used for writing down a **formula**. A formula shows how many **atoms** of each element are joined together. The formula for oxygen is O_2. The O stands for oxygen. The small 2 tells us that there are two oxygen atoms joined together. The formula for carbon dioxide is CO_2. The C stands for carbon. This shows that every carbon atom is joined to two atoms of oxygen.

Nitrogen dioxide, NO_2, is a **pollutant** in the air. It causes a brown haze. This is sometimes seen over large cities.

formula   symbols and numbers to show how elements are joined

Naming compounds

There are a few rules for naming **compounds** that contain a **metal**. Here they are:

• put the metal's name first

• the compound may contain only one **non-metal**. Write this down and change its ending to *ide*. For example, sodium and chlorine **react** to form sodium chloride.

• both oxygen and another non-metal could be in the compound. Then the ending of the non-metal's name ends in *ate*. Potassium **carbonate** contains potassium, carbon, and oxygen atoms.

No metal at all
Some compounds are made of two non-metals. They do not contain any metal. Then the second non-metal ends in *ide*. For example carbon monoxide and carbon dioxide are non-metal compounds.

Carbon dioxide is in these soft drink bubbles. "Di-" means two. So, carbon dioxide has two oxygen atoms.

This limestone is calcium carbonate.

Important compounds

Water in foods
Most foods contain water.

Food	Per cent water
Celery	94
Tomatoes	93
Spinach, raw	92
Strawberries	90
Apples	85
Bananas	76
Eggs, uncooked	74
Macaroni, cooked	72
Chicken, grilled	71
Beef, raw minced	54
Ham, cooked	54
Bread, wholewheat	35
Honey	15

Water is the most important **compound** on Earth. Without water all living things would die.

Water cycle
Water on the Earth is always moving. The Sun heats water in lakes and oceans. It changes to **water vapour**. The water vapour rises into the air. Then it cools and forms clouds. Inside the clouds tiny drops of water join to form bigger drops. These fall as rain, snow, or hail. Water runs off the land into rivers. This flows back into lakes and oceans. This is the **water cycle**.

Fresh fruit and vegetables are mainly water.

water cycle cycle of water from liquid to gas on Earth

Ores

Rocks often contain useful **metals**. These are called **ores**. Most ores are compounds of a metal and one or two **non-metals**.

Oxides, sulphides, and carbonates

An ore of a metal joined with oxygen is called an **oxide**. Copper oxide is an ore. An ore of a metal joined to sulphur is called a **sulphide**. Lead sulphide is an ore. A **carbonate** ore is a metal combined with carbon and oxygen. Magnesium carbonate is an ore.

Getting metal from ore

The **mineral** coke is a form of carbon. When coke is heated, it takes the oxygen from the metal oxide. The metal is left over.

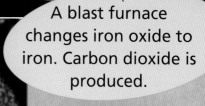

A blast furnace changes iron oxide to iron. Carbon dioxide is produced.

These cave paintings at Lascaux, France, were made using an iron oxide, called ochre.

ore metal that is combined with other elements

Uses of sulphuric acid

Sulphuric acid is a strong acid. It is the acid we use the most. This pie chart shows some of its uses.

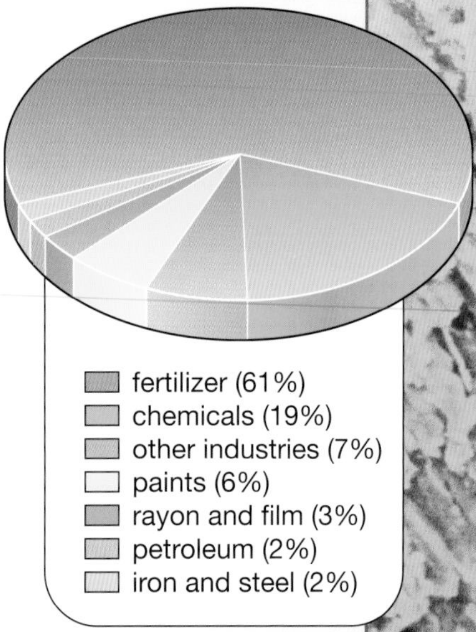

- fertilizer (61%)
- chemicals (19%)
- other industries (7%)
- paints (6%)
- rayon and film (3%)
- petroleum (2%)
- iron and steel (2%)

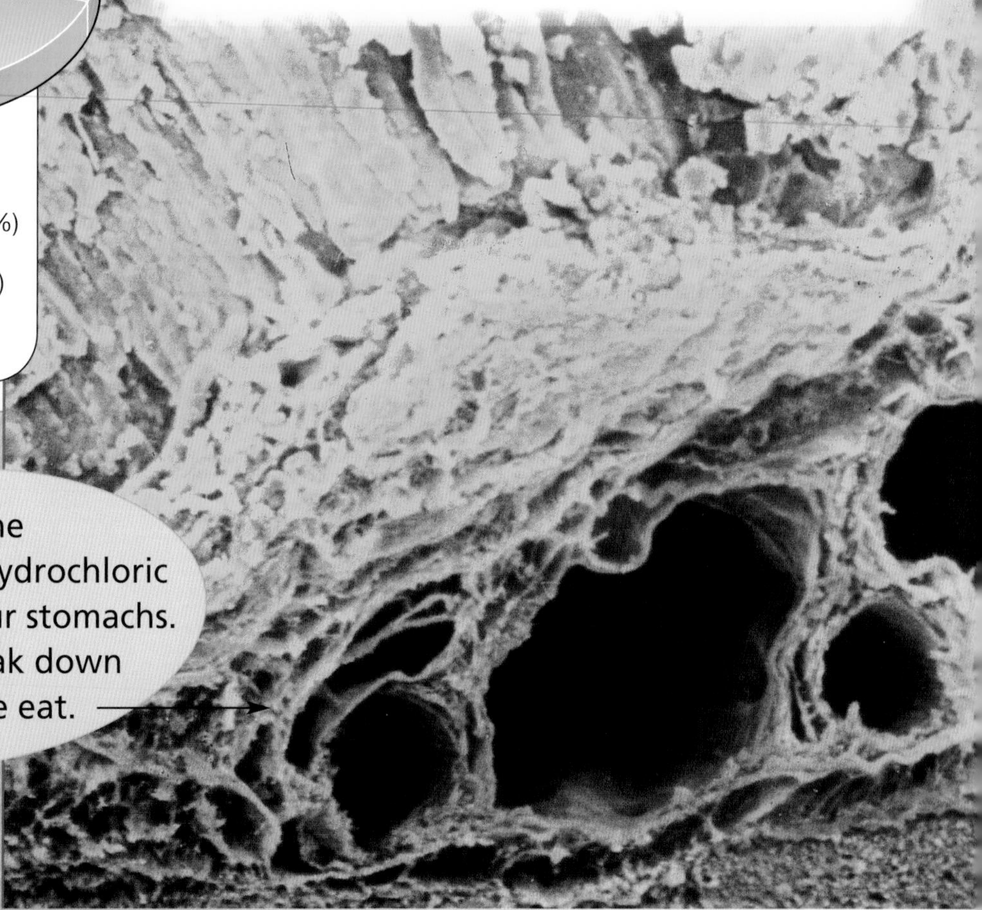

Acids

Acids are found everywhere. They taste sour. Many foods contain weak acids. Tomatoes and vinegar have acids in them. There are also weak acids in our body **cells**. They help to keep us alive and healthy.

Strong acids can burn our skin. They are **poisonous**. Hydrochloric acid is a strong acid. It is used for cleaning stone and swimming pools.

This is the stomach lining. Hydrochloric acid is found in our stomachs. It helps to break down the food we eat.

Word bank   acid compound that has a sour taste and can burn you

Bases

Bases are very common too. They have a bitter taste and feel slippery. Strong bases are **poisonous**. They can burn you badly. Sodium hydroxide is also called caustic soda. It is strong enough to **dissolve** bones. Strong bases are good for cleaning drains and ovens. But you have to be careful with them.

Calcium hydroxide is a weak base. It is used in medicines called **antacids**. Antacids help soothe upset stomachs. They **react** with stomach acid.

Desert soils

Desert soil contains a lot of bases. In deserts there is little rain to wash the bases away. Plants, like these cacti, can grow in the dry, basic desert soils. Many other plants cannot.

base compound that feels slippery and can burn you

Salts

Salts are common **compounds**. They form when an **acid reacts** with a **base**. Sodium chloride is the best known salt. It has thousands of uses. Only a small amount is used to put on food. Meat packers **preserve** meat with salt. Salt is used to make glass, treat leather, and to make other chemicals.

Other salts are important too. Ammonium chloride is used in batteries. Silver bromide is used in making film for cameras.

Epsom salts

Epsom salts are used for healing some skin rashes. They contain magnesium sulphate.

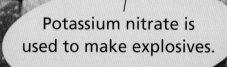

Potassium nitrate is used to make explosives.

Cellulose

Cellulose is found in plants. It is a kind of carbohydrate. Humans cannot break down cellulose. But some animals can break it down into sugar. Cattle and termites, like those above, can do this.

Compounds in living things

Nitrogen, oxygen, hydrogen, and carbon are found in **proteins**. Much of our body is made of protein. We need protein for growth. Meat, fish, and dairy products are sources of protein.

Carbohydrates are made up of carbon, hydrogen, and oxygen. Starch and sugar are carbohydrates. We need these for **energy**. Fruit, vegetables, and pasta contain sugar and starch.

Oils and fats are made up of carbon, hydrogen, and oxygen. We need them to keep our **cells** working. But too many can be harmful.

protein carbon compound that contains nitrogen; used for growth and repair in the body

Mixtures

Many fabrics are mixtures. Your shirt label tells you what the mixture is. It may say the fabric is cotton and polyester. The shirt fabric has properties of cotton. But it will have some of polyester too.

Most things around us are **mixtures**. Ocean water and fruit salad are mixtures. Mixtures are made up of several **pure substances**. But they are not held together by **chemical bonds**. They are separate. The pure substances in a mixture keep their own **properties**.

There are two types of mixture. Ocean water is one type. You cannot see the different parts. The other type of mixture has larger parts that you can see. Rocks and fruit salads are like this.

A mixture can contain **elements**, **compounds**, or both.

You can see this fabric is a mixture – of lycra and viscose fibres.

| element | mixture of elements | compound | mixture of compounds |

Separating mixtures

You can pick out the different parts in a mixture, if you can see them. Some mixtures contain solids of different sizes like rocks, pebbles, and sand. You can separate them by pouring the mixture through sieves with smaller and smaller holes.

Filtering can separate a sand and water mixture. The water passes through the filter paper and the sand is trapped.

Brushing with a mixture

Toothpaste is a mixture. The materials are evenly spread through it. But the materials in the toothpaste and their amounts vary. That is how different toothpastes can have different colours or flavours.

A mixture of sand, gravel, and other materials is mined at this gravel pit.

filter strain by pouring through paper or cloth

Solutions

Sugar seems to disappear when it is mixed in water. The pieces of sugar separate into sugar **molecules**. They are too small to be seen. We say the sugar **dissolves** in the water. This mixture is called a **solution**.

In a solution of sugar and water, the sugar molecules are spread evenly through the water. All solutions are like this.

Ocean water

Ocean water has a lot of solids dissolved in it. The pie chart below shows them.

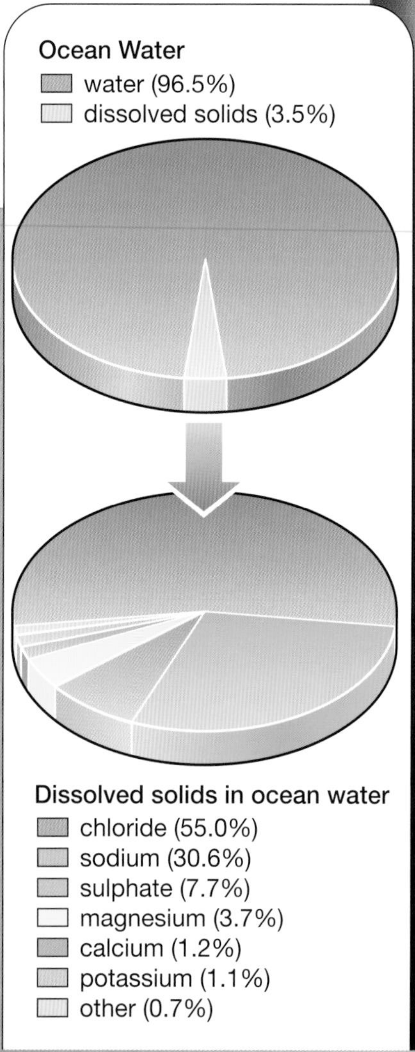

Ocean Water
- water (96.5%)
- dissolved solids (3.5%)

Dissolved solids in ocean water
- chloride (55.0%)
- sodium (30.6%)
- sulphate (7.7%)
- magnesium (3.7%)
- calcium (1.2%)
- potassium (1.1%)
- other (0.7%)

This shark is swimming in a solution. Ocean water has many substances dissolved in it.

dilute solution containing a small amount of material

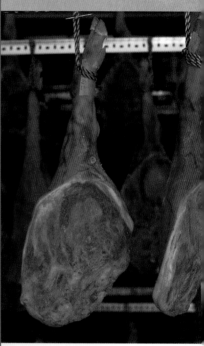

Stopping food going bad

Foods, like these hams, are **preserved** with salt. This removes water from the meat. Drier foods last much longer than fresh foods.

Describing solutions

Solutions can be weak or strong. A weak solution has a small amount of material dissolved in it. This is called a **dilute** solution. A strong solution has a large amount of material dissolved in it. This is a **concentrated** solution.

As you add more material to a solution, it gets more concentrated. Finally, no more material will dissolve. The solution is **saturated.**

Dissolving solids in liquids

A **solution** is usually made from a solid **dissolved** in a liquid. The solid can dissolve at different speeds. It depends on how big the pieces of solid are. The smaller the pieces are, the faster they dissolve. Stirring makes a solid dissolve faster too.

The temperature of the liquid affects how much solid will dissolve. Hot water will dissolve more sugar then cold water.

Adding salt to ice cream
Salt is added to the ice in an ice cream maker. This makes the water **freeze** at a lower temperature.

freeze change from a liquid into a solid

Dissolving gases in liquids

Gases, like ammonia and oxygen, dissolve in water. They form a solution. Ammonia water is used for cleaning. Oxygen dissolves in lakes and oceans. Fish breathe the dissolved oxygen in the water.

Unlike a solid, less gas will dissolve if it is warm. Fizzy drinks have carbon dioxide gas dissolved in them. A glass of soft drink soon goes flat in a warm room. This is because the solution loses carbon dioxide quicker.

Hot fish
Fish must have oxygen dissolved in their water. If the water becomes too warm, it loses oxygen. The fish might die.

You can see the **minerals** around the edges of this hot spring. The hot water is **saturated** with minerals. When it cools, the minerals come out of the water.

saturated containing as much substance as can be dissolved at that temperature

35

Dissolving liquids in liquids

Many substances **dissolve** in water. These include other liquids. Alcohol is a liquid that will do this. Antifreeze is a **solution** of water and alcohol. People put it in their car radiators. It stops the water in the radiator from **freezing**.

Not all liquids dissolve in water. For example, if you mix oil and water, oil floats on top of the water.

Making citrus oils

There is oil in the peel of lemons and oranges. The juice and oil is squeezed out of the fruit. The oil rises to the top of the juice. Then it is collected.

You should not use water to put out burning oils or petrol. They do not dissolve in water. Spraying water on them spreads the fire.

Separating solutions

It is not hard to separate the parts of a solution. You can separate a solid dissolved in a liquid just by leaving it in the air. The liquid will **evaporate** and leave the solid behind.

When a gas is dissolved in a liquid, you can heat the liquid. The gas escapes into the air. The liquid is left behind.

It is easy to separate solutions of liquids too. The **mixture** is heated slowly. Each liquid changes to a gas at a different temperature. As each liquid boils off, its gas is collected. The different parts of air are separated like this.

Air is cooled until it becomes a liquid. Then it is warmed up again very slowly. Nitrogen **boils** at a lower temperature than oxygen, so it turns into a gas first. This leaves oxygen behind. The two gases are collected separately.

Separating colours

In this photograph, ink from a marker pen was placed near the bottom of the filter paper. The ink was dried. The paper's bottom edge was placed so it just touched the liquid. The liquid moved up the paper. This separated the colours in the ink.

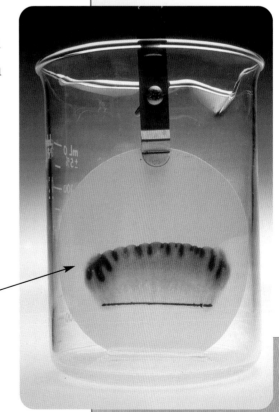

Black ink is made up of a mixture of colours. You can separate the colours like this. This method is called **chromatography**.

More mixtures

When you put pond water into a jar, it looks muddy. What happens when you let the **mixture** stand? Soil **particles** settle to the bottom of the jar. When soil particles do this they are called **sediment**.

Particles in a suspension

You can easily separate sediment from the liquid above it. You just pour the liquid off carefully. You do this at home when you pour off the liquid from a can of tuna fish.

This blood was spun at very high speeds. The suspended particles are pulled to the bottom of the tube.

A mixture of soil and water is a **suspension**. A suspension is a cloudy mixture of materials. It always separates out when left to stand.

Blood

Blood is a **solution**. Blood contains **dissolved** solids and gases. This is the yellow part.

Blood is also a suspension. Red blood **cells** and white blood cells are some of the solids suspended in the blood.

Fast water like this wears away bits of soil and rock from the land. These materials are suspended in the water.

Word bank   sediment solids not dissolved in a liquid; they fall to the bottom of the liquid

Separating suspensions

If you leave a suspension to stand, the particles will settle to the bottom. But large particles settle out more quickly than small particles. Sand and clay form a suspension in water. The sand settles to the bottom in minutes. The tiny clay particles will take hours to settle to the bottom.

You can separate a suspension quickly. You pour it through a **filter**. Filters are often made from paper. They have tiny holes. Particles that are larger than the holes cannot pass through. Most of our drinking water is filtered.

River deltas

A river carries lots of material called sediment. When a river empties into an ocean, it slows down. Then the materials settle to the bottom. Some rivers drop so much material that the sea cannot wash it away.

The red area is sediment. It forms new land called a delta. This is shaped like a fan and reaches into the ocean.

suspension mixture that contains a liquid in which particles settle after a time

Colloids

Whipped cream, fog, and smoke are all **colloids**.
A colloid is a **mixture**. Its **particles** do not separate
when it is left to stand, like they do in a **suspension**.
The particles in a colloid stay mixed. This is
because they are always bumping into one another.

The particles in a suspension are quite large.
The particles in a **solution** are tiny. The size of the
particles in a colloid are in between.

Cleaning with a colloid

A colloid is used to clean our water. Then it can be used again. The colloid looks like a fluffy gel. **Bacteria** and tiny particles stick to the gel and are trapped.

This is a sewage treatment plant. A colloid is used to trap bacteria.

Word bank colloid mixture with a particle size between that of solutions and suspensions

Kinds of colloids

Whipped cream is a colloid of a gas in a liquid. It is air in cream. Fog and clouds are colloids of a liquid in a gas. These are water droplets in air. Smoke is a colloid of solids in a gas, which is air. **Gels**, like jelly, are colloids of solids in a liquid.

Colloids can scatter light. If a beam of light is shone through a colloid, you can see it. Car headlight beams can be seen in fog. The water droplets in the air scatter the light.

Mixing milk
In fresh milk, the cream rises to the top of the bottle. Dairies break the cream into very small particles. The cream forms a colloid with the rest of the milk. Then it stays mixed. The milk is **homogenized**.

You can see this lighthouse beam. This is because of the tiny particles of dust and water in air.

Alloys

Mouth metals

Dentists use an alloy to fill holes in teeth. It is called **amalgam**. It contains mercury. When it is first made, amalgam is a liquid. But it hardens quickly.

Alloys are **mixtures**. They contain a **metal** and one or more other **elements**. Aluminium alloys are used to make aircraft. They are strong and lightweight.

Bronze is an alloy of copper and tin. Bronze is used for things that may come into contact with salt water. The tin does not **react** with the chemicals in seawater. Brass is an alloy of copper and zinc. It is used in musical instruments.

Word bank   alloy mixture of a metal and one or more other elements

Steel

There are many types of steel. They are all alloys of iron and other elements.

Different steels are made for different uses. Steel with manganese in it is very hard. It is used in railway tracks and military tanks. Stainless steel contains nickel and chromium. It is strong and does not **corrode**. Doctors use stainless steel tools for surgery.

Alloys of gold and copper are used to make jewellery. The copper adds strength to the gold.

Mending bodies

Alloys are used to mend broken bones as this X-ray shows. Stainless steel was used to make plates and screws. Now newer alloys are used instead. They are lighter and stronger than steel.

corrode damage by a reaction with chemicals

Find out more

Websites

BBC Science
News, features, and activities on science.
www.bbc.co.uk

Creative Chemistry
Fun, practical activities, quizzes, puzzles, and more.
www.creative-chemistry.org.uk

Skoool.co.uk
Help for science projects and homework.
http://kent.skoool.co.uk/

Books

Chemicals in Action: Elements and Compounds, Chris Oxlade (Heinemann Library, 2002)
Material World: Materials Technology, Robert Snedden (Heinemann Library, 2001)
Material World: Separating Materials, Robert Snedden (Heinemann Library, 2001)
Science Answers: Changing Materials, Chris Oxlade (Heinemann Library, 2003)

World Wide Web

To find out more about compounds, mixtures, and solutions you can search the Internet.
Use keywords like these:
- compounds +properties
- (name of a metal) +ore +mining
- mixtures +separating

You can find your own keywords by using words from this book. The search tips on the following page will help you find useful websites.

Search tips

There are billions of pages on the Internet. It can be difficult to find exactly what you are looking for. These tips will help you find useful websites more quickly:

- know what you want to find out about
- use simple keywords
- use two to six keywords in a search
- only use names of people, places, or things
- put double quote marks around words that go together, for example "chemical formulas"

Where to search

Search engine
A search engine looks through millions of website pages. It lists all the sites that match the words in the search box. You will find the best matches are at the top of the list, on the first page.

Search directory
A person instead of a computer has sorted a search directory. You can search by keyword or subject and browse through the different sites. It is like looking through books on a library shelf.

Glossary

acid compound that has a sour taste and can burn you

alloy mixture of a metal and one or more other elements

amalgam alloy that contains mercury

antacid medicine that contains a weak base and is used to soothe upset stomachs

atom tiny particle that makes up everything

bacteria tiny living things, so small you need a microscope to see them

base compound that feels slippery and can burn you

bleach remove colour with a substance

boil rapid change of state from a liquid to a gas. Takes place within the liquid and at its surface.

brittle firm to touch but easy to break

carbohydrate compound that contains carbon, hydrogen, and oxygen. It occurs in food and living tissues.

carbonate compound that contains carbon and oxygen

cell building block that makes up all living things

charge small amount of electrical energy

chemical bond strong attraction between two atoms

chemical property feature of something that tells us how it will react

chemical reaction change that produces one or more new substances

chemical symbol short way of writing the name of an element

chromatography method used to separate colours in a mixture or a dye

colloid mixture with a particle size between that of solutions and suspensions

compound substance made of two or more different types of atom joined together

concentrated solution containing a large amount of material

corrode damage by a reaction with chemicals

covalent compound compound formed when atoms join and share electrons

crystal solid that has particles arranged in a regular, repeating pattern

dilute solution containing a small amount of material

dissolve mix completely and evenly

electron tiny, negatively charged particle outside the nucleus of an atom

element substance made from only one kind of atom

energy ability to cause change

erupt when a volcano shoots out lava

evaporate change from a liquid to a gas

filter strain by pouring through paper or cloth

formula symbols and numbers to show how elements are joined

freeze change from a liquid to a solid

gel colloid of solids in a liquid

geyser opening in the Earth that shoots up water and steam from underground

homogenize break cream into tiny particles so that they do not separate from the milk

ion atom or group of atoms with an electric charge

Latin ancient language used by the Romans

mass amount of matter in an object

matter anything that takes up space and has mass

melt change from a solid to a liquid

melting point temperature at which a solid turns into a gas

metal material that is shiny and lets heat and electricity move through it easily

metalloid element with some properties of both metals and non-metals

mineral non-living solid material

mixture material made of elements or compounds not joined chemically

molecule two or more atoms held together by chemical bonds

neutron particle with no charge, found in the nucleus of an atom

non-metal element without properties of metals

nucleus centre of an atom, made of protons and neutrons

ore metal that is combined with other elements

oxide compound formed when oxygen joins up with another element

particle tiny bit

physical change change in how something looks, not in what makes it up

physical property feature that can be seen or measured without changing what a substance is made of

poisonous substance that will harm you

pollutant harmful substance in the air, water, or on the land

preserve stop from going bad

property feature of something

protein carbon compound that contains nitrogen. It is used for growth and repair in the body.

proton positively charged particle in the nucleus of an atom

pure substance matter that is the same throughout

react take part in a chemical reaction and produce one or more new substances

room temperature about 20 °C (68 °F)

rust iron oxide, formed when iron reacts with oxygen in the air

salt compound formed when an acid reacts with a base. Sodium chloride is a common salt.

saturated containing as much material as can be dissolved at that temperature

sediment solids not dissolved in a liquid; they fall to the bottom of the liquid

solution mixture in which one material dissolves in another

state of matter whether something is solid, liquid, or gas

sulphide compound that contains sulphur

suspension mixture that contains a liquid in which particles settle after a time

ultraviolet (UV) light invisible light that is beyond violet in the spectrum and causes skin to burn

water cycle cycle of water from liquid to gas on Earth

water vapour water in a gas state

Index

Titles in the Freestyle Express: Material Matters series include:

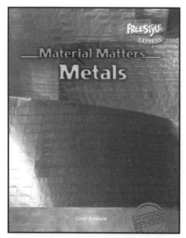

Hardback   1 844 43356 0

Hardback   1 844 43357 9

Hardback   1 844 43358 7

Hardback   1 844 43381 1

Hardback   1 844 43382 X

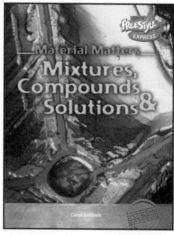

Hardback   1 844 43601 2

Find out about other Freestyle Express titles on our website www.raintreepublishers.co.uk

The Night
Before Christmas

BY CLEMENT MOORE

illustrated by TOMIE DE PAOLA

Oxford University Press

Oxford University Press, Great Clarendon Street, Oxford OX2 6DP

Oxford New York
Athens Auckland Bangkok Bogota Bombay
Buenos Aires Calcutta Cape Town Dar es Salaam
Delhi Florence Hong Kong Istanbul Karachi
Kuala Lumpur Madras Madrid Melbourne
Mexico City Nairobi Paris Singapore
Taipei Tokyo Toronto Warsaw

and associated companies in
Berlin Ibadan

Oxford is a trade mark of Oxford University Press

© Tomie de Paola 1980
First published by Holiday House, New York
First published by Oxford University Press 1981
Reprinted 1983, 1987, 1991
First published as paperback 1982
Reprinted 1984, 1986, 1988, 1989, 1991, 1996
Reprinted in paperback with new cover 1997

British Library Cataloguing in Publication Data
Moore, Clement Clarke
The Night before Christmas.
1. Santa Claus — Poetry   2. Christmas poetry
3. American poetry — Juvenile
I. Title   II. De Paola, Tomie
811'.2   PS2429.M5N5
Paperback ISBN 0-19-272131-3

Printed in Hong Kong

FOR ALL MY NEIGHBORS

W. F. '80   T. deP.

'TWAS
the night before Christmas,
when all through the house
Not a creature was stirring,
not even a mouse;

The stockings were hung
by the chimney with care,
In hopes that St. Nicholas
soon would be there;

The children were nestled
all snug in their beds,
While visions of sugarplums
danced in their heads;

And Mamma in her 'kerchief,
    and I in my cap,
Had just settled our brains
    for a long winter's nap;

When out on the lawn
   there arose such a clatter,
I sprang from the bed
   to see what was the matter.
Away to the window
   I flew like a flash,
Tore open the shutters
   and threw up the sash.

The moon on the breast
of the new-fallen snow,
Gave the lustre of midday
to objects below,
When, what to my wondering
eyes should appear,

But a miniature sleigh,
    and eight tiny reindeer,
With a little old driver,
    so lively and quick,
I knew in a moment
    it must be St. Nick.

More rapid than eagles
    his coursers they came,
And he whistled, and shouted,
    and called them by name;
"Now, *Dasher!* Now, *Dancer!*
    Now, *Prancer* and *Vixen!*
On, *Comet!* On, *Cupid!*
    On, *Donder* and *Blitzen!*
To the top of the porch!
    To the top of the wall!
Now dash away! Dash away!
    Dash away all!"

As dry leaves that before
    the wild hurricane fly,
When they meet with an obstacle,
    mount to the sky;
So up to the housetop
    the coursers they flew,

With the sleigh full of toys,
and St. Nicholas too.
And then in a twinkling,
I heard on the roof,
The prancing and pawing
of each little hoof—

As I drew in my head,
   and was turning around,
Down the chimney St. Nicholas
   came with a bound.

He was dressed all in fur,
    from his head to his foot,
And his clothes were all tarnished
    with ashes and soot;
A bundle of toys
    he had flung on his back,
And he looked like a pedlar
    just opening his pack.

His eyes—how they twinkled!
　　His dimples, how merry!
His cheeks were like roses,
　　his nose like a cherry!
His droll little mouth
　　was drawn up like a bow,
And the beard of his chin
　　was as white as the snow;

The stump of his pipe
    he held tight in his teeth,
And the smoke it encircled
    his head like a wreath;
He had a broad face
    and a little round belly,
That shook when he laughed,
    like a bowlful of jelly.

He was chubby and plump,
    a right jolly old elf,
And I laughed when I saw him,
    in spite of myself,
A wink of his eye
    and a twist of his head,
Soon gave me to know
    I had nothing to dread;

He spoke not a word,
  but went straight to his work,
And filled all the stockings;
  then turned with a jerk,
And laying his finger
  aside of his nose,
And giving a nod,
  up the chimney he rose;

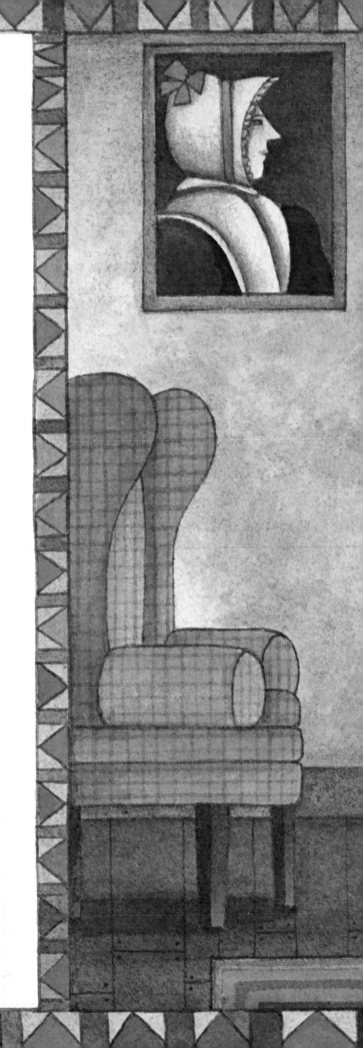

He sprang to his sleigh,
  to his team gave a whistle,
And away they all flew
  like the down of a thistle.

But I heard him exclaim,
 ere he drove out of sight,
"Happy Christmas to all.
 And to all a good night."

About This Edition

Clement Moore, who was a professor at General Theological Seminary, wrote *The Night Before Christmas* for his children in 1822. The poem was originally called *A Visit from St. Nicholas* and was first published in the newspaper, *Troy Sentinel*, in 1823.

Tomie de Paola has set the poem in the 1840's, using his own home in a small New Hampshire village as a model. His borders are based on designs from New England quilts, many of which he owns.